This simple book is dedicated
To my wonderful bride, Debby
(who is amazing!)
and to my four fantastic kids:
Luke, Elise, Abby and Hunter.

Although I have my times of
"catness," I trust overall I've made
God famous in your eyes.

(Special thanks go to Gerald Robison and all my supporters
for their ideas and input!)

The theme of this book is based on the
notable differences between what may be
two of mankind's (if not God's)
favorite creatures: cats and dogs.

Knowing that there are animal lovers of each,
we hope that no one takes offense at our
acknowledging the different traits of these
beloved creatures. For certainly no offense is intended.
Rather, we merely recognize that the God-given traits
of cats and dogs can be similar to certain
theological attitudes held by many Christians.

In nature, these attitudes are suitable to both felines and
canines. But in our theology, some attitutudes may draw us
closer to God, and others actually pull us away from Him.

We hope you learn to differentiate these attitudes,
and, as a result, draw closer to God who delights in you-
as well as in cats and dogs!

A dog says,
"You pet me, you feed me,
you shelter me, you love me,
You must be God."

A cat says,
"You pet me, you feed me,
you shelter me, you love me,
I must be God!"

How Cats And Dogs View God

Cats And Dogs Having Quiet Times

Cats And Dogs In A Worship Service

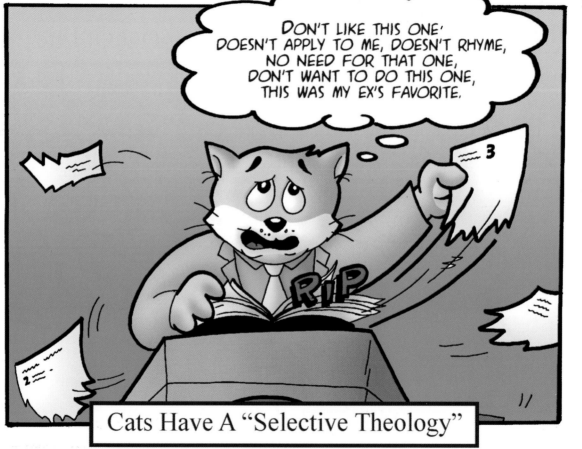

Cats Have A "Selective Theology"

What Cats And Dogs Delight In

12

Cats Love To "Protect" Their Church

13

Where Cats And Dogs
Run When They're Afraid

How Cats And Dogs See God's Four Seasons

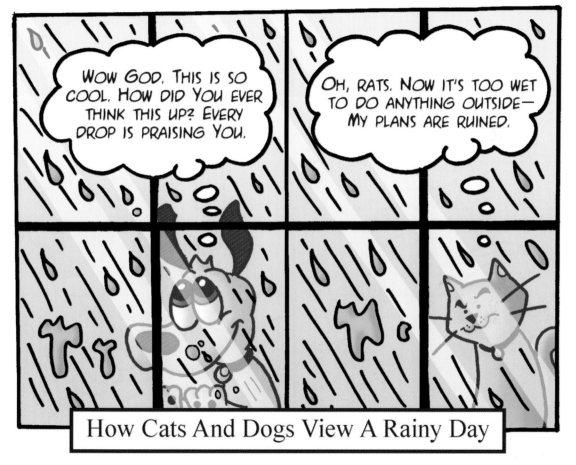

How Cats And Dogs View A Rainy Day

Cats And Dogs Know Their Rightful Place

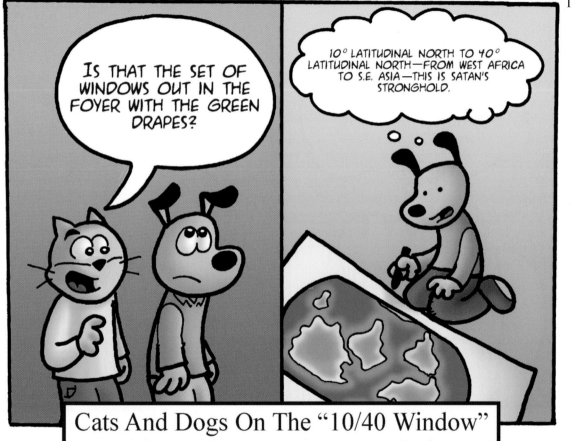

Cats And Dogs On The "10/40 Window"

Cats Serve God How They Want.
Dogs Serve God How He Wants.

Cats And Dogs Take Risks Differently

Cats And Dogs Prepare Differently
For The "Game Of Life"

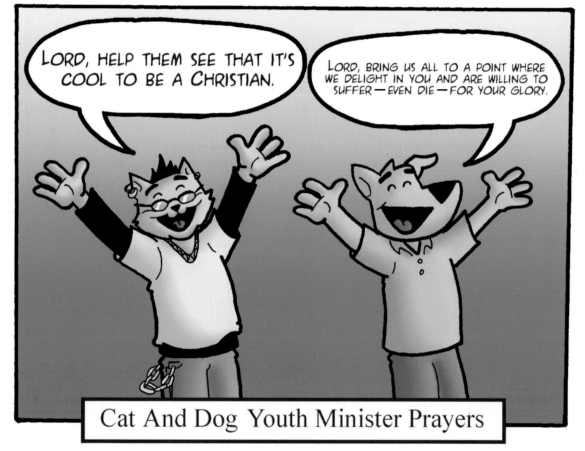

Cat And Dog Youth Minister Prayers

When The Offering Plate Comes Around

How Cats And Dogs Choose Churches

28

When Pastors Don't End On Time

What Cats And Dogs
First Read Each Morning

What Cats And Dogs Are Thinking Right Before The Sermon Starts

When Too Much Change Is Given

Responding To Trials

36

Praying For Believers
Going Through A Divorce

How They Know They Are Believers

Responding To God's
Heart For The Nations

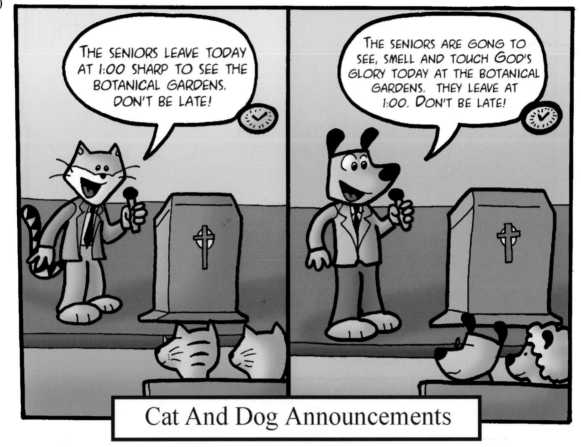

Cat And Dog Announcements

Cat And Dog Greeters

42

Church Potlucks

Cats And Dogs Can Agree
For Different Reasons

How Cat And Dog Pastors Respond To A Request To Do A Sunday Morning Outreach

Mission Chairpersons Responding To A Request To Have "Perspectives" Missions Course For Their People

Cats And Dogs Watching Sunsets

When Cats And Dogs Are Forced To Miss The Prayer Meeting At Church

How Cats And Dogs Respond
To Their Pastor's Teaching

What Cats And Dogs Say To Missionaries

Preparation For The
Upcoming Missions Conference

54

How Cats And Dogs
Strategize To Reach The Youth

57

On Relating To Job's Kids

58

Responding To A One To Two Week "Hug Team"
To Help Orphaned Children In Mozambique*

*TO FIND OUT MORE ABOUT "LEAST OF THESE" MINISTRY, E-MAIL BECKY BATES @RBATES1074@AOL.COM

Cat And Dog Grandparenting

How Cat And Dog Elders
Respond To Change

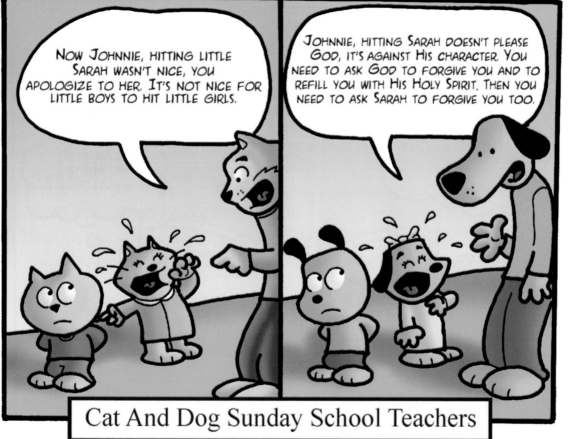

Cat And Dog Sunday School Teachers

Seeing Jesus In The Large Glass Picture

Ending The Church Prayer Meeting

64

Pastoral Goals

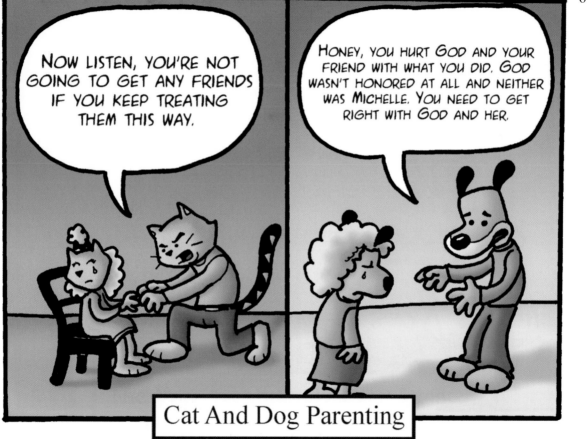

Cat And Dog Parenting

Positions On Homosexuality

Attitudes Toward Work

Regarding The Lottery

Church Mission Statements

Mission Conference Speakers

Starting New Church Plans

Worship Leaders Choosing Songs

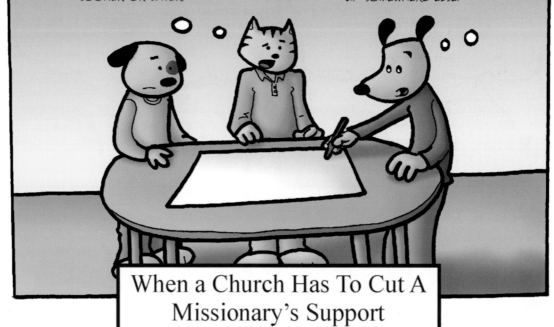

When a Church Has To Cut A Missionary's Support

Cats And Dogs On The Athletic Field

At Christmas Time

How They View Technology

Starting Gossip

82

Praying After 9/11

Praying Through The War On Terror

Watching The News

The Number Of Verses That Relate
To The Great Commission

What Cats And Dogs Do On A
Cold, Wet Sunday Morning

Regarding Captured Terrorists

Surrendering Before God

At Men's Conferences

Visions Of Heaven

After Receiving An Inheritance

Cats React In Their Giving.
Dogs Prayerfully Plan.

Crisis Management

On Human Resources

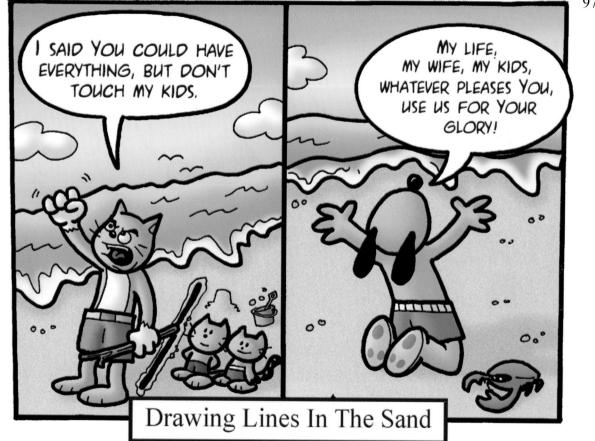

Drawing Lines In The Sand

Cats Try To Fit God Into Their Busy Life.
Dogs Fit A Busy Life Around Their Times With God.

After A Major Disaster